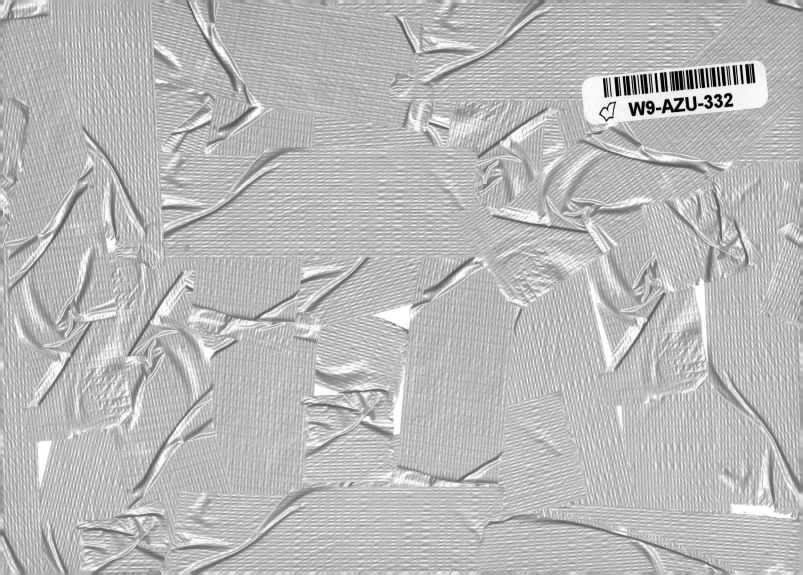

W9-AZU-332

THERE, I FIXED IT

(No, You Didn't)

Other books by the Cheezburger Network

I Can Has Cheezburger? A LOLcat Colleckshun
Fail Nation: A Visual Romp Through the World of Epic Fails
How to Take Over Teh Wurld: A LOLcat Guide 2 Winning
Graph Out Loud: Music. Movies. Graphs. Awesome.
I Has a Hotdog: What Your Dog Is Really Thinking
Teh Itteh Bitteh Book of Kittehs: A LOLcat Guide 2 Kittens

THERE, I FIXED IT

(No, You Didn't)

Cheezburger Network

**Andrews McMeel
Publishing, LLC**

Kansas City • Sydney • London

Andrews McMeel Publishing, LLC
an Andrews McMeel Universal company
1130 Walnut Street, Kansas City, Missouri 64106

www.andrewsmcmeel.com

11 12 13 14 15 TEN 10 9 8 7 6 5 4 3 2 1

ISBN: 978-1-4494-0059-0

Library of Congress Control Number: 2010930545

ATTENTION: SCHOOLS AND BUSINESSES
Andrews McMeel books are available at quantity discounts with bulk purchase for educational,
business, or sales promotional use. For information, please e-mail the Andrews McMeel Publishing
Special Sales Department: specialsales@amuniversal.com

CONTENTS

KLUDGE-O-METER

Most of you will read this book for a good laugh or a cringe, but a few of you—the same ones who scoff in the face of live electric wires in puddles and blithely ignore the "Do Not Try This at Home" warnings—well, we know what you're going to do. But we just couldn't sleep at night if we didn't at least give you some warning.

So the fancy folks over in No Lawsuit Land cooked up this scale. It seems pretty self-explanatory. Should you inevitably end up in the local ER, please remember to have a family member bring the book. That way, the surgeon will know the extent of your injury and the size of your badge of honor. Note: Do *not* bring the book yourself, or the blood may soak in and make the pages hard to read.

duct taped   jury rigged   epic kludge

THERE, I FIXED YOUR BATHROOM

Accurate representation of where bottled water comes from.

duct taped · jury rigged · epic kludge

FIX SPOTTER ROB:

Here is how my friend fixed his shower after receiving complaints that the hot water wasn't working so well.

duct taped   jury rigged   epic kludge

FAVORITE COMMENT

Slapchop says, "I've seen these before. They're for washing your hands. There is usually a little white bar of soap lying at the bottom for your convenience."

duct taped   jury rigged   epic kludge

Fireman says, "By the way, there is something to be said for a toilet with armrests."

duct taped   jury rigged   epic kludge

Even the Blob cares about personal hygiene.

duct taped   jury rigged   epic kludge

"Running water" is a relative term.

duct taped　　　jury rigged　　　epic kludge

FIX SPOTTER DIZ: Good to see they recycle plastic bags.

duct taped   jury rigged   epic kludge

Billy says, "Something very bad must have happened for this to be put in place."

duct taped   jury rigged   epic kludge

9

Ad said house has an indoor pool.

duct taped   jury rigged   epic kludge

FAVORITE COMMENT

Mary says, "There, I mixed it!"

duct taped   jury rigged   epic kludge

FIXER SCOTT: Keeps it from hitting me in the head when the water is shut off.

duct taped   jury rigged   epic klu

Oh God, why wouldn't you flush
before taking the picture?!

duct taped   jury rigged   epic kludge

13

Toilet liked wall so much
he put a ring on it.

FIXER KERRY: This is how to
keep a toilet from running!

duct taped   jury rigged   epic kludge

FIXER NATHAN: It looked real nice when I wrapped it with duct tape, but I forgot to get a picture.

duct taped

jury rigged

epic kludge

15

FIXER ROB: Cost $87 and took me ninety minutes from tear-out to finish.

duct taped   jury rigged   epic kludge

FIX SPOTTER KELLY:
We can't afford two trash cans . . . and this way, we'll have room for one big one!

duct taped   jury rigged   epic kludge

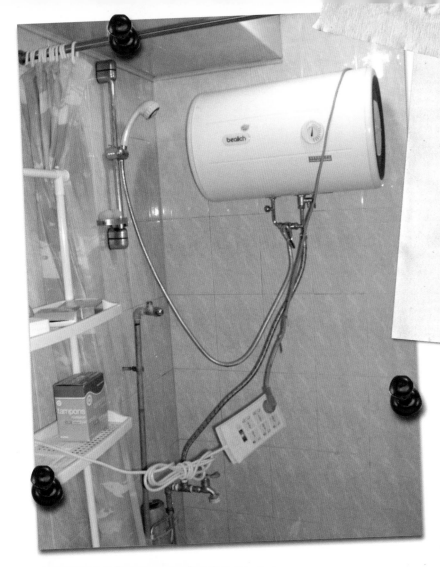

Dear Landlord,
Please stop trying to kill me.

duct taped   jury rigged   epic kludge

Place it over a
fire hydrant for
an instant bidet!

duct taped   jury rigged   epic kludge

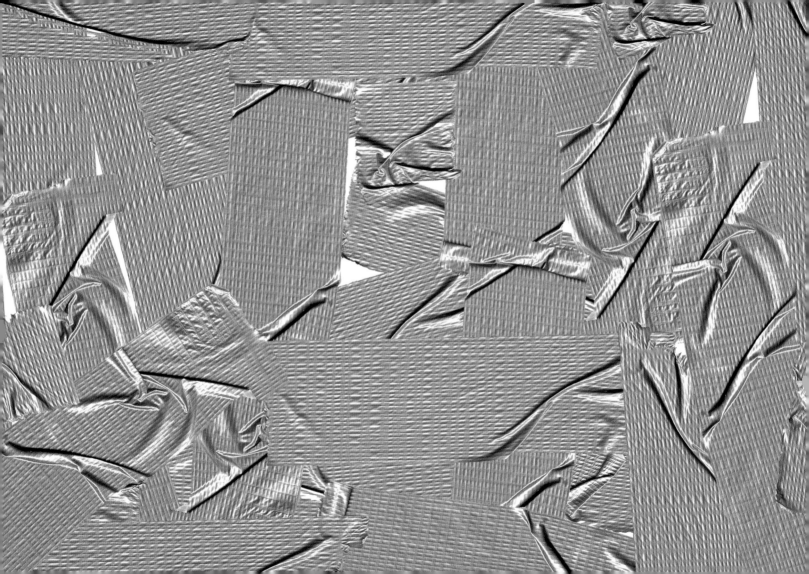

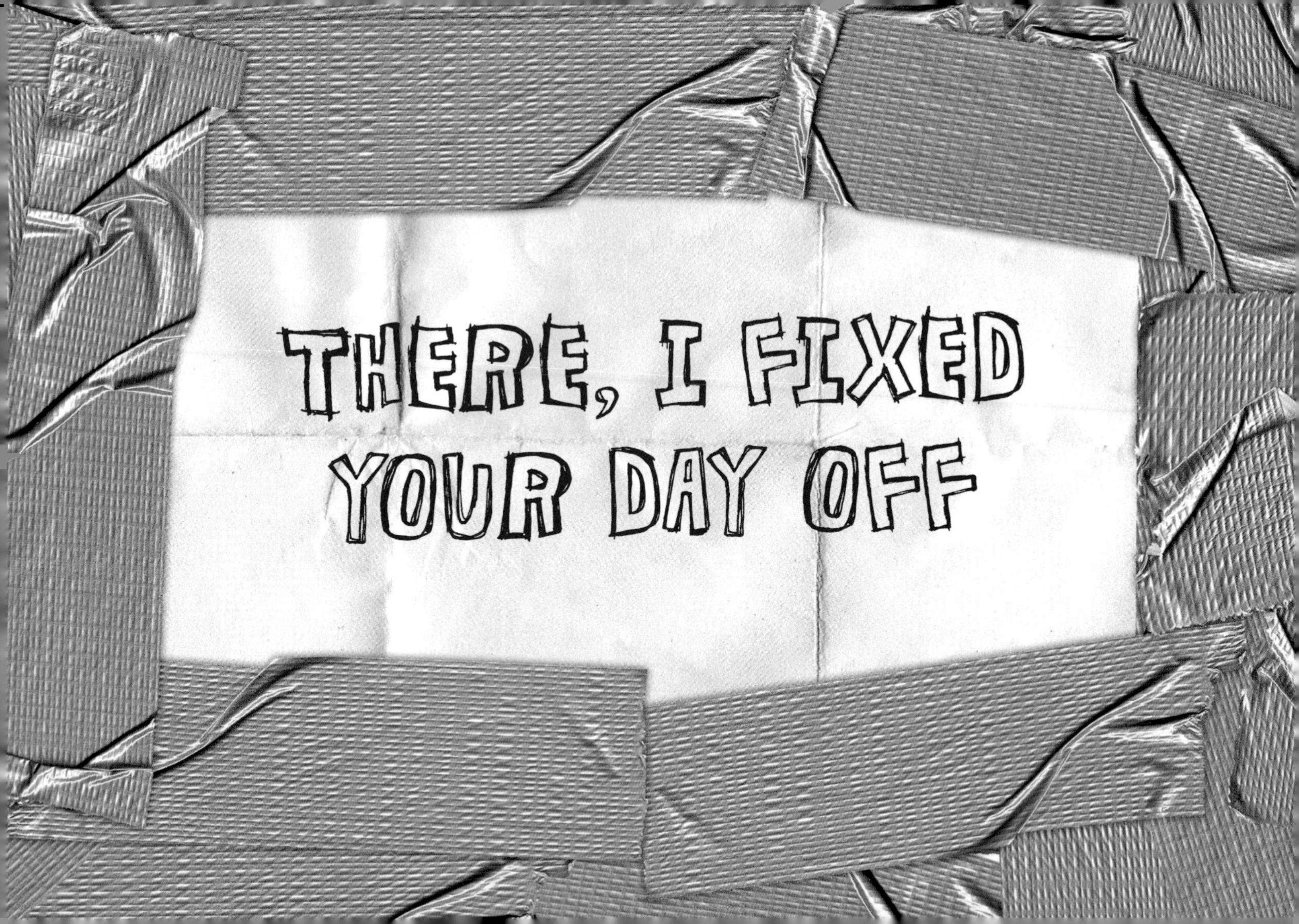
THERE, I FIXED
YOUR DAY OFF

Barbecue will not be thwarted by Thor.

duct taped   jury rigged   epic kludge

FAVORITE COMMENT

Demetrius says, "In Whoville, they say, the Grinch's TV grew three sizes that day!"

duct taped   jury rigged   epic kludge

FIX SPOTTER BOB: Beer holder, umbrella, ashtray recliner. Found this at the Gorge campground after the Dave Matthews Band show.

duct taped   jury rigged   epic kludge

duct taped   jury rigged   epic kludge

They really have some cutting riffs. They slice up the competition.

25

And they said Espionage 101 was a worthless class.

duct taped   jury rigged   epic kludge

FIXER ROGER: I use this fix to fly my favorite airplanes, the Harrier and E. E. Lightning in Flightgear. Can't believe nobody else does this—it's so obvious!

duct taped   jury rigged   epic kludge

FIXER JIM: Practical solution for frozen margaritas while camping.

duct taped   jury rigged   epic kludge

You'll need instructions after
all that tequila.

duct taped   jury rigged   epic kludge

FREE
PICKS

Make your own right here

This machine accepts
**ALL
CREDIT
CARDS**

SAFETY CLUB

duct taped   jury rigged   epic kludge

NatureGeek24 says, "Uh—credit card . . . musician . . . ? Does anyone else see the problem here?"

Bridge says, "We don't have a seven solid ball. But it's OK! We'll mark out the ten striped and call it seven solid. But then we won't have a ten striped. We'll just use the five solid. But what about the five solid? We'll use the eight ball—dear God, when does the madness end?!"

duct taped   jury rigged   epic kludge

Could you slow down a bit, dear? The jostling is making Mulder blurry.

duct taped   jury rigged   epic kludge

FIXER KATHERINE: My mom wanted my hair to be curly for prom, so she duct taped a hair dryer to a microphone stand and put my head underneath it.

duct taped   jury rigged   epic kludge

33

THERE, I FIXED YOUR DINNER

Makeshift pancake warmer. Bonus: air freshener!

Moxie Man says, "No, you don't understand. It's currently maple sap season here in the Northeast. They've flushed the coolant out of this car and replaced it with maple sap. Once enough sap boils off, it will ooze out of the pinholes in the heater core, through the vent, and directly onto the pancakes! It's brilliant!"

duct taped   jury rigged   epic kludge

36

FIXER NEAL: Constant turning ensures an even toast!

duct taped   jury rigged   epic kludge

37

FIXER ALEX: My coffee pot fell off the table the other day and shattered. I went to the store to buy a replacement. Ten dollars for a replacement, you say? Preposterous! I could buy a new coffee maker for that much, but I wasn't about to throw out the perfectly good one I had at home. So I looked around the apartment for something to fix it. An old teapot and a fork was all I needed. I wedged the fork there to disengage the antidrip feature.

duct taped   jury rigged   epic kludge

duct taped   jury rigged   epic kludge

Delicious
Thaase
Food

"Fusion cuisine"
has gone too far
this time.

FIX SPOTTER DREW: The greatest thing
to happen to beer since ice.

duct taped   jury rigged   epic kludge

When data storage becomes obsolete,
use your bookcase (see page 87) as a
fabulous grill!

duct taped   jury rigged   epic kludge

Some men are just big babies.

duct taped   jury rigged   epic kludge

43

Thadius says, "In Soviet Russia, iron is full of food!"

duct taped   jury rigged   epic kludge

FIXER MARY: Never underestimate the creativity of college students who want their dorm fridge at max holding capacity.

duct taped   jury rigged   epic kludge

I sure hope those aren't pot brownies,
or this is about to be a long night.

duct taped   jury rigged   epic kludge

46

FAVORITE COMMENT

Whodatlzz says, "Now every bottle is a screw-off cap."

duct taped   jury rigged   epic kludge

See, honey? you don't need a stand mixer.

duct taped   jury rigged   epic kludge

FIXER MIKE: This is what I did when the control board went out on the microwave. What could have been a $200 repair cost me less then $10 to fix. I just had to wire the interior light, turntable motor, cooling fan, and high-voltage transformer to the light switch. Flip it on and start microwaving, then flip it off when done.

duct taped   jury rigged   epic kludge

Coffee isn't addictive.
Why would you say that?

duct taped   jury rigged   epic kludge

JimDawg says,
"Weld a gun rack
to it and put a
remote on it, and
no man could
resist buying one."

MowBQ

06.07 18:14

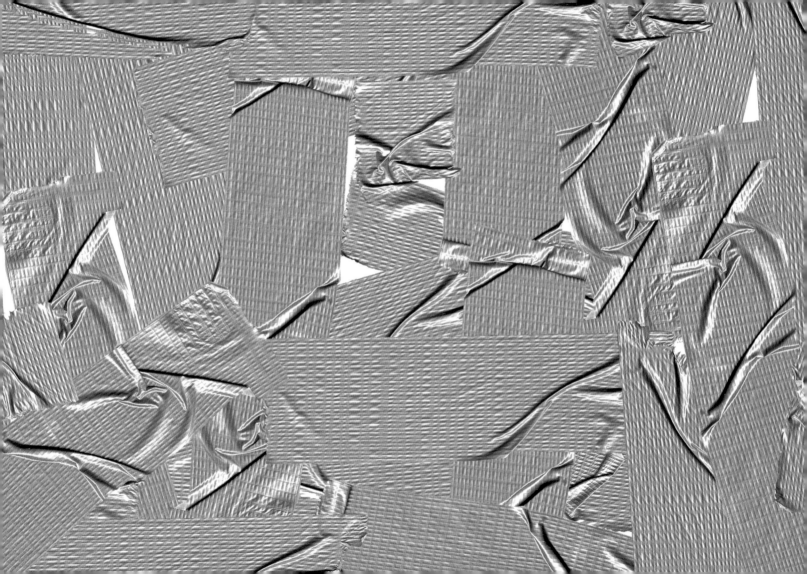

THERE, I FIXED
YOUR HOUSE

Glad to see they're taking the necessary steps to fix the problem.

Rehevkor says, "They're retractable steps to be used in the event of door-to-door salesmen or Jehovah's Witnesses (redundant, I know). A trapdoor leading to the shark-infested cellar will be added later."

duct taped   jury rigged   epic kludge

One man's trash is another man's flower arrangement.

 duct taped

 jury rigged

 epic kludge

The 1601 is the number of times this mailbox has been backed into.

duct taped   jury rigged   epic kludge

FAVORITE COMMENT

Kc/cc says, "This guy seems to be uncertain about what to do here. Apparently, he's feeling optimistic that it will stay up since all that glassware is currently stored underneath on the countertop, but not quite confident enough to actually let the cabinet hold things. What I do know is that finals better be over already."

duct taped   jury rigged   epic kludge

This looks like a trap.

duct taped   jury rigged   epic kludge

58

Because nothing says "tasteless" like an uncovered lightbulb.

duct taped   jury rigged   epic kludge

The bicycle lock lets potential robbers know you're not to be messed with.

60

duct taped   jury rigged   epic kludge

FIX SPOTTER DWIGHT: I debated for two years whether or not to paint my own house. I decided against buying a $400 ladder to do the job myself and elected to hire a couple of guys I assumed would have the tools to do the job. I was wrong.

duct taped   jury rigged   epic kludge

Tetris creator's college dorm room.

duct taped · jury rigged · epic kludge

c/o Fluidmaster Nightwhirl
3100 Stonehenge Lane

duct taped   jury rigged   epic kludge

Homeowners' insurance doesn't cover chiropractic care.

duct taped   jury rigged   epic kludge

64

FIX SPOTTER KEREN: My grandmother Pila from Chile put together this amazing sprinkler system!

duct taped   jury rigged   epic kludge

The brick is really there to keep the barbecue from escaping into another yard.

duct taped   jury rigged   epic kludge

duct taped   jury rigged   epic kludge

FIXER JOE:
That new storm
door really spruces
up the place!

67

Nom nom nom-doors love popcorn ceilings.

duct taped   jury rigged   epic kludge

Hard hats required.

duct taped jury rigged epic kludge

Great—the ceiling light is drunk again.

FAVORITE COMMENT

Zac_upp says, "And here we see the rare Ceiling Fan Cocoon. Soon its wings will burst forth as the fan in the back already has."

duct taped   jury rigged   epic kludge

Four-wheel drive mandatory.

FAVORITE COMMENT

Thomas Westgard says, "It's a boat ramp. When the tide comes in, it's fine."

duct taped   jury rigged   epic kludge

81

Billy wanted a new bike.
Mom wanted free labor.

duct taped   jury rigged   epic kludge

450

Yarr! Let's be piratin' this mailbox.

duct taped   jury rigged   epic kludge

THERE, I FIXED YOUR OFFICE

Office needs a new ruler? I'll pencil in your request.

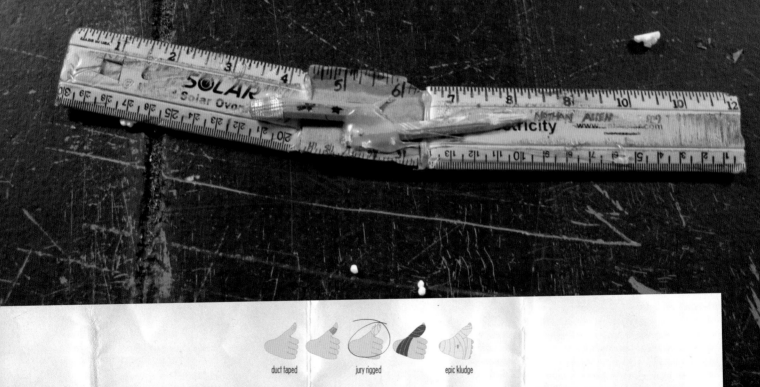

duct taped   jury rigged   epic kludge

FAVORITE COMMENT

Alleycat says, "It's a Java Server."

duct taped

jury rigged

epic kludge

When cloning a new dolly wouldn't
work, zip ties were the only option.

duct taped   jury rigged   epic kludge

Fanboy Wife says, "Does this just prove that we never outgrow the desire to build forts?"

duct taped   jury rigged   epic kludge

MWahatten says, "Is there *anything* a staple puller can't do? Being a pretend dinosaur, eating paper, drinking water, biting humans, and even pulling staples! I love those little critters."

duct taped

jury rigged

epic kludge

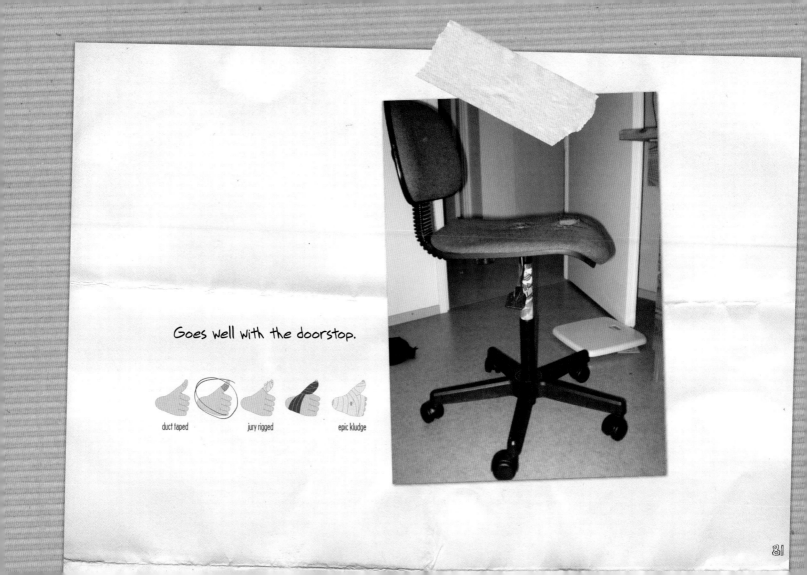

Goes well with the doorstop.

duct taped   jury rigged   epic kludge

There, I faxed it.

duct taped   jury rigged   epic kludge

FAVORITE COMMENT

Dono1 says, "It's pitiful to have your computer supported by a childlike platform. But enough about Windows Vista; take a look at those cool LEGOs!"

duct taped   jury rigged   epic kludge

FIXER STEVE: It's ninety degrees in my office. The place has been buttoned up all weekend with the AC off, and the ones we have in this part of the former barn are inadequate. *Plus*, the one near me is blocked by filing cabinets and a divider. So I went to Lowe's with the company credit card and bought some dryer hose and duct tape.

duct taped   jury rigged   epic kludge

The break is a lie.

duct taped   jury rigged   epic kludge

old data storage.

duct taped   jury rigged   epic kludge

And they say Styrofoam is not recyclable!

duct taped   jury rigged   epic kludge

FIXER ROBERT: I fixed the problem of having an office in my car.

DLZ says, "Chat log: 'omg i just got pulled over. let me point the webcam out the window so you can see the cop lol lol.'"

duct taped

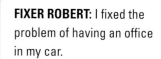
jury rigged

epic kludge

Best!
Weekend!
Ever!

duct taped   jury rigged   epic kludge

Derelict says, "Well, that's one way to stay on top of your job."

duct taped   jury rigged   epic kludge

duct taped   jury rigged   epic kludge

FIXER JANET: It's a high-tech monitor stand (with a custom enclosed cat feature).

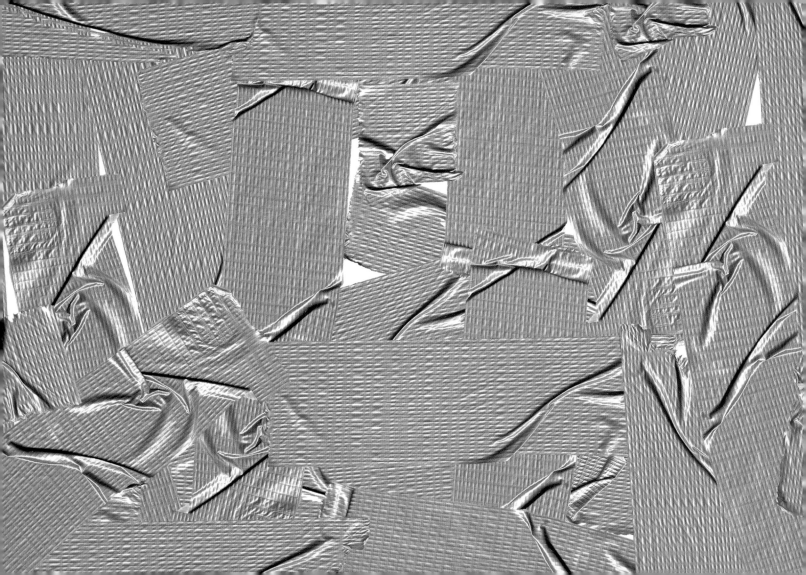

Piku says, "Well, if blatant lies are the theme, how about 'One lady owner, full service history.'"

Reply: Pat says, "Only drove it to church on Sunday."

Completion: Ray says, "Oh, look—she's left her hymn book in the glove compartment!"

duct taped   jury rigged   epic kludge

iMuffler

duct taped   jury rigged   epic kludge

It's getting more and more difficult to avoid major spoilers.

duct taped   jury rigged   epic kludge

78

FIXER ANTON: I didn't feel like rebuilding it.

jury rigged   epic kludge

FAVORITE COMMENT

Husabob says, "Was this done to prevent the steering wheel from being wrenched from the driver's hands on bad roads?"

duct taped

jury rigged

epic kludge

Bicycle Kludged
for two.

duct taped   jury rigged   epic kludge

Piku says, "SRS—
Suddenly Released
Staples."

duct taped   jury rigged   epic kludge

Fuel efficiency
is getting silly.

duct taped   jury rigged   epic kludge

FIX SPOTTER STEVEN:
Objects in mirror may be
younger than they appear.

duct taped   jury rigged   epic kludge

FIX SPOTTER DAVID:
Saw this car in Chicago near Indiana. I was trying to figure out what the metal was attached to the window. It looks like old air-conditioner parts.

duct taped   jury rigged   epic kludge

Bike baskets are for the birds.

106

duct taped   jury rigged   epic kludge

Houseboat for any budget.

duct taped   jury rigged   epic kludge

107

FAVORITE COMMENT

Bruce says, "The owner was attempting to increase the resale value of his car by going from a four-door to a six-door."

duct taped   jury rigged   epic kludge

Health-
conscious bike
does "reverse
tricycle" yoga
pose.

duct taped   jury rigged   epic kludge

Finally found a use for all those free AOL CDs.

duct taped · jury rigged · epic kludge

110

FIXER JOE: The kids cracked the rudder on our paddleboat. I haven't been able to find a replacement for the life of me. I cut one out of plywood with a jigsaw and had one made out of Plexi, but neither would stand up. Plexi was too brittle; the wood warped and wore out. My brothers-in-law, a doctor and a manager at a media company, came up with a $5 solution. Yes, that's a cutting board. It's made of a durable polymer with just the right amount of flex, and it was only $5. Ridiculous, but it worked.

duct taped   jury rigged   epic kludge

What's next, a park bench? Actually, that's not a bad idea . . .

duct taped   jury rigged   epic kludge

Dono1 says, "This economy has been hard on everybody— especially Santa."

duct taped   jury rigged   epic kludge

Looks like your car is having a bad day. You two should talk it out. Let it vent a little.

duct taped   jury rigged   epic kludge

Putting the "fix" in Fixie.

duct taped   jury rigged   epic kludge

FAVORITE COMMENT

Daniel says, "What do you mean 'no storage capacity'? With a roll of duct tape, you can tape a ton of stuff on that hood."

duct taped   jury rigged   epic kludge

FIX SPOTTER ANDREW: The picture was taken in an apartment parking lot in College Station, Texas—the home of Texas A&M, one of the best agriculture and mechanical engineering schools in the country.

duct taped   jury rigged

epic kludge

FAVORITE COMMENT

Slapchop says, "The plastic lawn furniture seat says it's unpretentious; the mountain bike tires say it's got that rugged, go-anywhere attitude. (Actually it looks like a great idea—traditional wheelchairs are expensive.)"

duct taped   jury rigged   epic kludge

Taking "going green" a little too far, don't you think?

duct taped   jury rigged   epic kludge

FAVORITE COMMENT

Sarah C. says, "If only it would stop trying to sell pot to kids on the playground, it could be a respectable car."

duct taped   jury rigged   epic kludge

FIXER DARREN: Here is a picture of my Jeep Cherokee. I fixed it properly after hitting a deer, and then I hit another deer. So I fixed it again, for free this time. Haven't even had a close call with a deer since.

duct taped   jury rigged   epic kludge

Hey! You can't
take those
off the lot!

duct taped

jury rigged   epic kludge

Goya: the champagne of headlights.

duct taped   jury rigged   epic kludge

FIX SPOTTER JOHN:
Dude said it works.
Don't want to find out.

duct taped   jury rigged   epic kludge

124

You know you need to see a mechanic when your car's trim starts attempting suicide.

duct taped

jury rigged

epic kludge

To keep that fresh "new car" smell from fading.

duct taped · jury rigged · epic kludge

FAVORITE COMMENT

Wideaperture says, "It's not a sound system, it's a court-ordered sobriety test—like a breathalyzer ignition lockout, only for geeks. 'Please enter your thirteen-digit StarCraft CD key to start the car.'"

duct taped

jury rigged

epic kludge

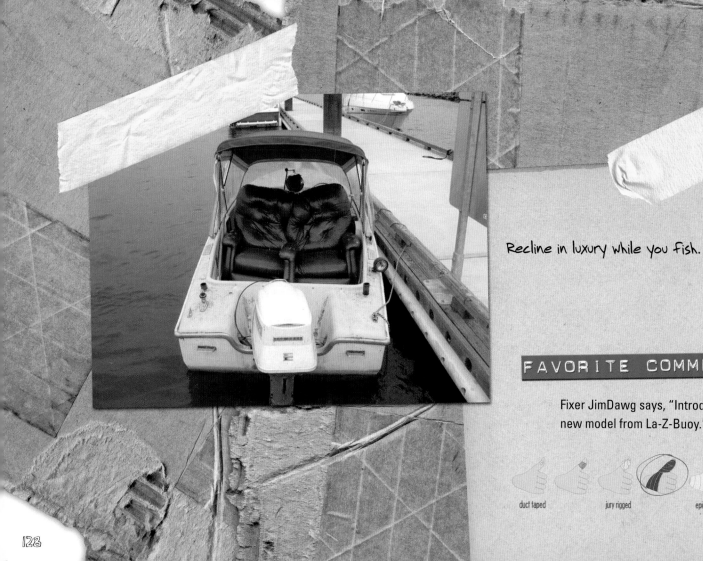

Recline in luxury while you fish.

FAVORITE COMMENT

Fixer JimDawg says, "Introducing the new model from La-Z-Buoy."

duct taped   jury rigged   epic kludge

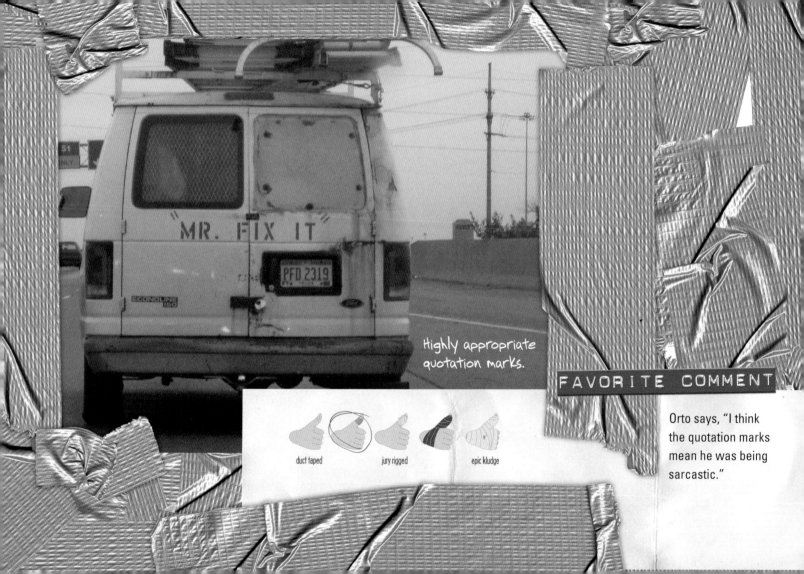

"MR. FIX IT"

PFD 2319

ECONOLINE 150

Highly appropriate quotation marks.

duct taped   jury rigged   epic kludge

FAVORITE COMMENT

Orto says, "I think the quotation marks mean he was being sarcastic."

FIRE DEPARTMENT ON SPEED DIAL

Daniel says, "Props to these guys. I hate it when I am walking my fire around in a wheelbarrow and smoke gets in my eyes. Next time I am using a fan to blow the smoke away from me."

duct taped   jury rigged   epic kludge

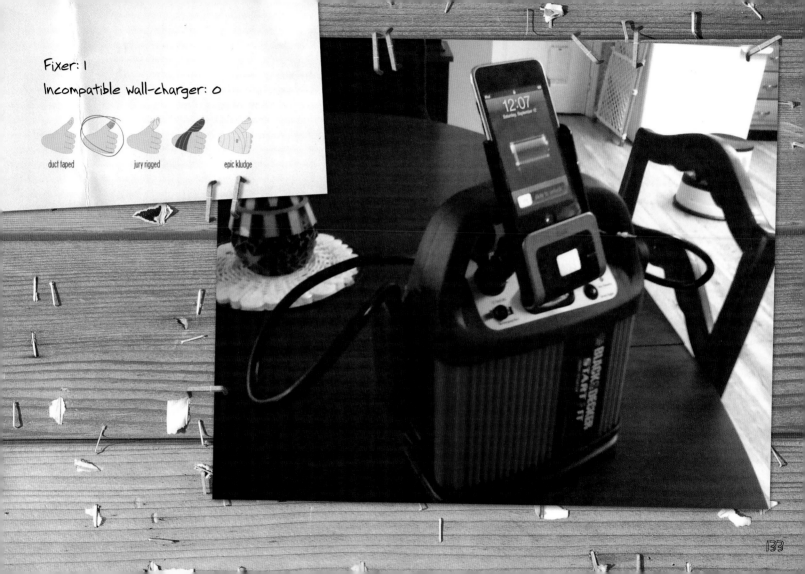

Fixer: 1

Incompatible wall-charger: 0

duct taped   jury rigged   epic kludge

FIXER JONAS: It's from 2006, when the Wii just came out and we couldn't get any component cables for months. So I wired that shit up myself.

duct taped   jury rigged   epic kludge

FIXER PETER: I guess a normal person would have turned the knob on the TV itself, but I took a different approach to fix the problem.

duct taped   jury rigged   epic kludge

135

Rob says, "The sharpener that makes *all* pencils go 'Number 2.'"

duct taped   jury rigged   epic kludge

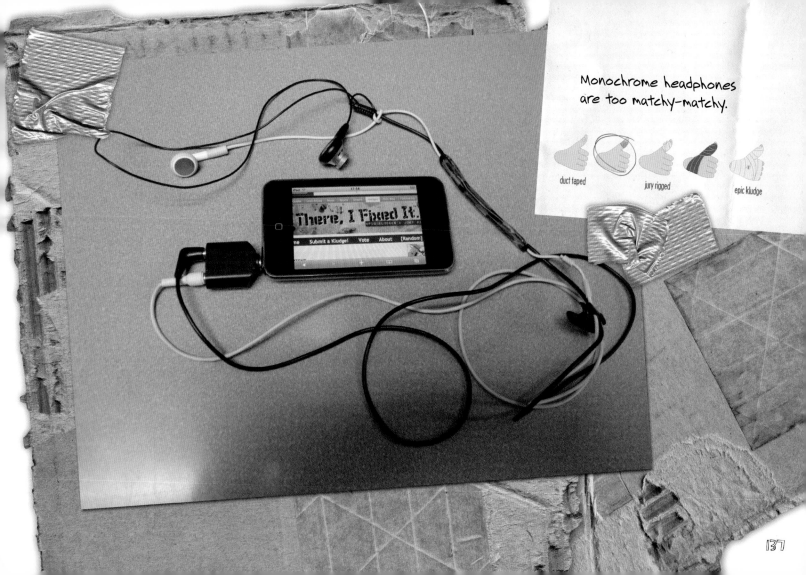

Monochrome headphones
are too matchy-matchy.

duct taped   jury rigged   epic kludge

Laundry day
for the Red Hot
Chili Peppers.

duct taped   jury rigged   epic kludge

Fixer: 2

Incompatible wall-charger: 0

duct taped   jury rigged   epic kludge

Fixed that forkin' thing!

duct taped   jury rigged   epic kludge

140

FIXER CHRIS: My feckin' cheap-ass phone had a semibroken charge port; it needed a constant downward force for it to charge, so—voilà.

duct taped

jury rigged

epic kludge

FAVORITE COMMENT

TechBender says, "After consulting the accountant for a third time, Steven decided on the cheaper hurricane simulator."

duct taped   jury rigged   epic kludge

FIXER JIM: This is an ad-hoc camera tripod that I made by making two cuts in a mailing box from the car trunk and weighing the flaps down with boots. I was on a photo scavenger hunt, and we only got full points if every team member was in each photo. Sometimes there was no one around to help!

duct taped   jury rigged   epic kludge

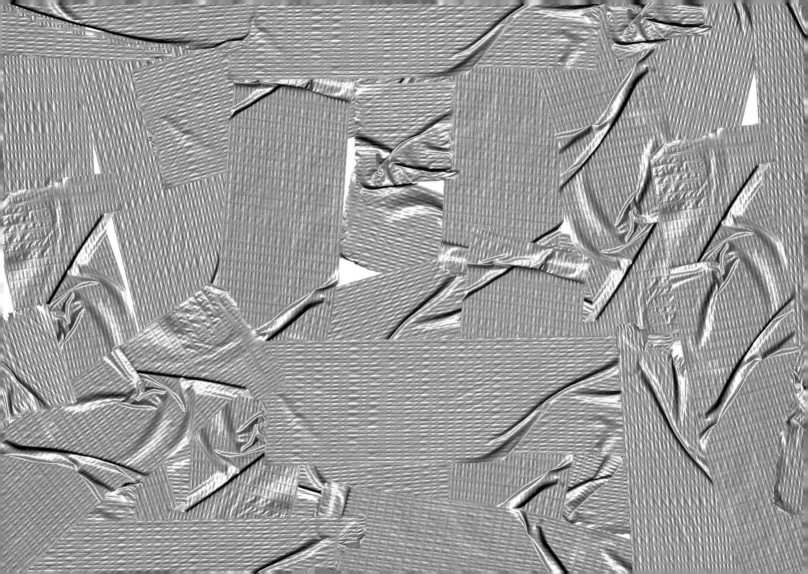

DUCT TAPE
HERO

Naw, it blends right in.
Dad'll never notice.

duct taped   jury rigged   epic kludge

Yeah, because you looked awesome in braces.

duct taped   jury rigged   epic kludge   147

Wait, wait, wait—is this like the two gargoyle heads? One always tells the truth, and one always tells a lie, and I can only ask one gargoyle one question? But with sinks, obviously.

duct taped

jury rigged

epic kludge

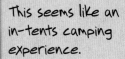

This seems like an in-tents camping experience.

duct taped   jury rigged

epic kludge

The parasite will latch onto the host, eventually merging with the body until even biologists can't discern where one ends and the other begins.

duct taped   jury rigged   epic kludge

Anna Rexia says, "Blew Insurance Money on ~~Tape~~ Crack."

duct taped   jury rigged   epic kludge

FIX SPOTTER IAN: What to do when faced with a shattered eight-foot mirror? Don't even bother with duct tape; this is a lightweight job, and painter's masking tape will do the trick!

duct taped   jury rigged   epic kludge

Rag top: you're doing it wrong.

duct taped   jury rigged   epic kludge

163

FIX SPOTTER NICK: Here's a photo I took when I was in Poland a couple of years back. We were wandering along a mountain road when we spotted this power pole in disguise. I guess they didn't want to cut down the tree, so they just strapped another tree to it and wrapped it all up in masking tape.

duct taped   jury rigged   epic kludge

NASCAR opens the Soccer Mom 500 Division.

DON'T WORRY— THE CITY WILL FIX THAT!

But still no bukkits.

NEW SEAL

AND OLD WALRUSES

duct taped   jury rigged   epic kludge

duct taped   jury rigged   epic kludge

World's largest Jenga game.
Winner gets a free year of gas.

FIX SPOTTER JOE: The winter was brutal this year in Lewisburg, West Virginia, and the roof of the State Department of Transportation gas station took a larger than usual load of snowfall. This temporary fix prevented further damage to the structure, which has now been repaired.

159

DIY pole wears a unique outfit to prom.

duct taped   jury rigged   epic kludge

Sidewalk closed for traffic cone meeting.

duct taped   jury rigged   epic kludge

Honestly, who throws away a perfectly good umbrella? Mary Poppins is rolling in her grave.

duct taped   jury rigged   epic kludge

FIX SPOTTER SARAH: This is a photo I took in summer 2007 in Bryson City, North Carolina. I can only guess that the town decided to "fix" erosion on the Tuckasegee River by shoring it up with old rusted-out car bodies.

duct taped   jury rigged   epic kludge

FIX SPOTTER CHRIS: Wurzburg's solution to parking on tight roads—just paint the lines on the sidewalk!

duct taped · jury rigged · epic kludge

When the city refuses to make a
four-way stop, concerned suburbanites
take matters into their own hands.

duct taped   jury rigged   epic kludge

FIX SPOTTER MIKE: We were on holiday in Scotland, and I came across a lamppost that had been fixed with a nonfluorescent bulb. If you look even closer, only one wire is connected!

duct taped   jury rigged   epic kludge

You have to tree them with respect. If they parked further away, they'd be bushed.

duct taped   jury rigged   epic kludge

This looks legit. You kids have fun.

duct taped   jury rigged   epic kludge

After losing everything in the flood, a family of cones comforts one another on the street.

duct taped   jury rigged   epic kludge

FIX SPOTTER CLAIRE: It started out with just the shopping cart and was later upgraded with the mattress and trash can.

Just because they live under bridges doesn't mean trolls don't have decorative taste.

FIX SPOTTER ADAM: Well, I personally didn't fix it, but I sure feel better about the bridges in Westfield, Massachusetts, after seeing this gem.

duct taped   jury rigged   epic kludge

Nice try, Kite-eating Tree,
but I'm not as gullible as
some blockheads.

duct taped   jury rigged   epic kludge

FIX SPOTTER PAGE: In case you live on a river but just gotta have your satellite TV.

duct taped jury rigged epic kludge

173

I see Google Maps has
started making street signs.

duct taped   jury rigged   epic kludge

Gargomon says, "So, when this rack eventually falls down, does that mean it 'kicked the bucket'?"

duct taped

jury rigged

epic kludge

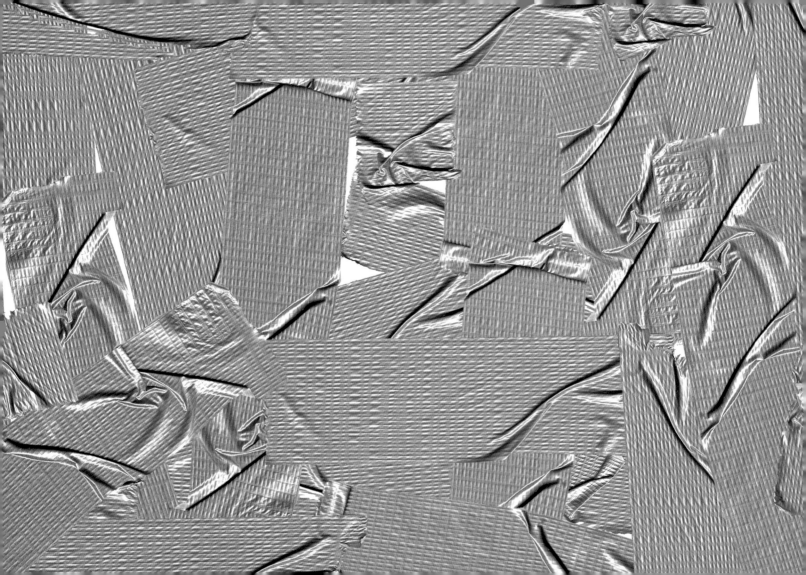

I CAN HAUL ANYTHING! WATCH!

Here we see a flock of wild Fragile Cargo banding together to take down large prey.

duct taped   jury rigged   epic kludge

They want how much
to rent a truck?
Oh, hell no.

duct taped   jury rigged   epic kludge

Wow, there must be at *least* $5 in cans there.

duct taped   jury rigged   epic kludge

yeah, I've been working out. You can't see it in my arm yet, but look how long I can hold this up.

duct taped   jury rigged   epic kludge

With all those other modes of transport, I kind of hope they're disguising a flying car.

duct taped   jury rigged   epic kludge

duct taped   jury rigged   epic kludge

Ah, one-handed driving.
The only thing better is . . .

Look, Ma! No hands!

duct taped   jury rigged   epic kludge

Looks like they kept packing even after they took the kitchen sink.

duct taped   jury rigged   epic kludge

PRO TIP: Keep your AC unit in place by resting it on a bottle of antifreeze.

duct taped   jury rigged   epic kludge

187

For preventing canoe leaks, of course.

duct taped   jury rigged   epic kludge

It's sad to see such a pretty truck force herself into a corset for the sake of society.

duct taped   jury rigged   epic kludge

ABOMINEERING

razor
+ tape
+ wrench
—————————
= back shaver

Shave
PARTAVAAHTO
Raklodder

duct taped   jury rigged   epic kludge

$$\frac{\text{pothole} + \text{sign}}{= \text{solid road}}$$

duct taped   jury rigged   epic kludge

2 plastic forks + 2 plastic knives + spool of thread + rubber bands = salad tongs

duct taped   jury rigged   epic kludge

golf umbrella
+ broomstick
+ lots of rope
————————————
= beach umbrella

duct taped   jury rigged   epic kludge

duct tape
+ file folders
———————————
= fridge compartments

duct taped   jury rigged   epic kludge

Ford Taurus
+ box fan
———————————
= redneck turbo charger

duct taped   jury rigged   epic kludge

RFEC

197

stick
+ scissors
+ rope
―――――――――
= hedge clipper

FAVORITE COMMENT

WhiteBelly says, "Kites! I hate kites! Flyin' around all high on themselves. I'll show 'em."

duct taped   jury rigged   epic kludge

old phone
+ eraser
+ broken cigarette lighter
+ 30 rubber bands
───────────────
= desk charger

duct taped   jury rigged   epic kludge

chain
+ grocery bag
_____
= secure bike lock

duct taped   jury rigged   epic kludge

plastic bags
+ packaging material
+ toilet paper wrapper
= shower curtain

duct taped   jury rigged   epic kludge

dead tree
+ hose clamp
+ strapping
_____
= mailbox post

duct taped   jury rigged   epic kludge

$$\frac{\text{hole}}{+\ \text{leaf}}$$
$$= \text{glass}$$

duct taped   jury rigged   epic kludge

sheet
+ cord
+ bedpost
———————
= fitted sheet

...uct taped   jury rigged   epic kludge

yard + ??? = profit

duct taped   jury rigged   epic kludge

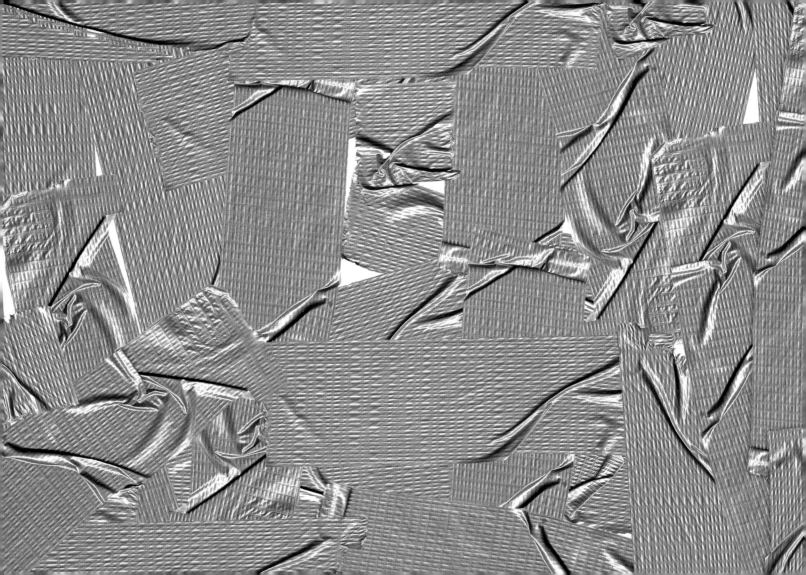

CREDITS

PRODUCTION CREDITS

Writing and Editing: Sonya Vatomsky, Donna "Ms. Fix-It" DeRonde, Todd Sawicki, and Ben Huh

Fix-It Illustrations: Emily Nokes

IMAGE CREDITS

There, I Fixed Your Bathroom . . . 1

Not Street Legal . . . 95

I Can Haul Anything! Watch! . . . 177

Abomineering . . . 191